# Own Your Time & Space

# By Corey Camp

# &

# Jimmy "The Blueprint" Williams

# Own Your Time & Space

## By Corey Camp

## &

## Jimmy "The Blueprint" Williams

No part of this book may be reproduced, distributed, or transmitted in any form or by any means, or stored in a database or retrieval system, without written permission from the publisher. Sale of this book without the front cover may be unauthorized. If this book is without the front cover, it may have been reported to the publisher as "unsold or destroyed" and neither the author (s) nor publisher may have received payment for it.

**Published by**

**Moji House Publishing LLC.**
**PO Box 39776**
**Philadelphia P.A. 19106**

# **<u>Contents</u>**

## *Part I (Time)*

1) Acknowledgements from Corey

2) Acknowledgements from Jimmy

3) Preface

4) The Language of Time

5) Time and Education

6) Social Issues and Time

7) Lifespan and Time

8) Religion Over Time

9) Price vs. Value

10) Time and Technology

11) Random Thoughts about Time

## *Part II (Space)*

12) My Relationship With Space

13) Space and Education

14) Social Issues and Space

15) Price vs Cost vs Value

16) Big Mac & A Bible

17) Technology and Space

18) Solutions: Don't Be A Mutombo

19) About The Author (Corey)

20) About The Author (Jimmy)

# Acknowledgements from Corey

Here is the time I think I should pay homage to those who made sure I got a pristine education. I'll start with my beautiful mother who told me education was my job. She introduced me to multiple types of educations. My formal education was my job but, my environmental education and my traveling education were provided by her. She made sure that if I did my job, I could travel. She allowed me to play individual and team sports and she paid for ALL of it. My environments were generally controlled and my trips paid for, even if it meant struggle for her. To my mother, I say THANK YOU, with all my love. To my immediate family that always had my back, whether it was a fight with a neighborhood child, or being there so my mom could work weird hours, to teaching me the skills they had so I could be diverse. They did it all. To my 3rd grade teacher Mrs. Porter who made Black History a priority. She taught Black History all year and was the first person to tell me Black History shouldn't be just one month a year. To Mr. Thompson, who in 6th grade, told me I was going to be great. His philosophy was do it correctly or do it again. To Mr. Bussey

and my grandmother Ora Lee Camp
who were my elders and taught me
about the history of the neighborhood I
lived in and the history of the city.  Both
lived through the Great Depression,
World Wars, and the Jim Crow South.
They took the time to give me a sense of
pride in the History of my people that
most young people never learn.  To Ms.
Linton in Middle School who gave me
the phrase "I laugh and I joke, but I do
not play."  I still live by that phrase.
 Lastly Mr. Morlitz, the principal of my
Middle School, that helped me get me
into Central High when my attendance
said no way and Dr. Pavel, the Principal
of Central High, who kept me in that

prominent academic environment when my actions said to give up on me.

Thank you both for judging the full me and not just the defiant part.

# Acknowledgements from Jimmy

This masterpiece is dedicated to my family. I love you all. I don't want to name everyone because it would make the book too long and we don't want a long body of work. I always find it interesting how Mothers get all the amazing songs and dedications. I mean you have "I'll always love my momma" by The Intruders, there's "Sadie" by The Spinners which was also bodied by R. Kelly, "Dear Momma" by Tupac, "A Song for Mama" by Boyz II Men, and countless other dedications and shot-outs. While I appreciate women and understand why we celebrate them, I want to take this time to thank all of the Black Men who have helped shape me and make me the man I am. As I travel through life, I realize my circumstances and blessings were not shared by everyone. I meet people who have never had a positive male in their life and I have been fortunate to have many. This book is dedicated to those men. My father JW Sr (RIP), My two Grandfathers Buck, and Big John (RIP), Uncle John aka Blaze (RIP), Uncle Quincy aka Uncle Q, Uncle Ronnie, Uncle Mike, Uncle Manfred, Cousin Mark, and Robert Thurston. Whether they know it or not I have learned from all of these men whether it was what to do or what not to do. Also to all of my male teachers and mentors which are too many to name I say thank you.

What's interesting is by growing up with so many males present in my life I surround myself with men who are also present for the next generation. So to all of my homies and my baby brother Kyree the internet troll who is also an amazing father who show the kids the Loafs on a daily basis I say thank you.

# **Preface**

If you study Ancient Egyptian History you will see time and space as a topic of discussion. All throughout History, you will see time and space having significant importance but never discussed as it will be in this book. This book was born out of hours and hours of conversation between my co-author Corey and myself. Corey and I have had conversations since our days at the Legendary Central High School in Philadelphia of which both of us belong to the 254th graduating class. We became friends because of our interest in sports, but what I soon realized was that Corey was brilliant. He is literally one of the smartest people I know. This was an early lesson in not judging a book by it's cover. Corey was a street guy. Now I don't mean that in any negative way. I'm not calling him a thug or a super predator like Hillary Clinton might (No Shots) but it was obvious he was from the streets but also had an amazing mind. Just as an FYI, there is a difference in being "from" the streets and being "of" the streets. Corey was so smart that he would ace classes in one of the most difficult academic environments without attending class. He was too busy gambling or playing cards (LOL). He would tutor and help

9

people with classes he didn't attend.

Now that's enough of me giving Corey props I feel uncomfortable (LOL). I say all that just to let people understand that these conversations have been going on for decades at this point because we are old AF.

One theme that continually comes up in our conversations is me speaking on the importance in space and Corey talking about the importance of time. Understand that when I speak of space I am speaking of land. Land and space will be used interchangeably in this book. He has interesting perspectives that I thought needed to be shared. I have always wanted to write a self-help/philosophy book because I'm a fan of the genre and because I also have the nerve to think people want to hear what I have to say. I hope those that support us will take something from this body of work and engage us in conversation and give us their opinions on this body of work.

Corey: Twitter: @AboveAvgSavage
 IG: @254CoreyCamp

Jimmy: @JWTheBlueprint

*If you are reading the physical book you may see some sentences underlined and in bold. Those are hyperlinks for the kindle version and also something you may want to look up.*

# _Part I: Own Your Time_

# _By_

# _Corey_

# <u>The Language of Time</u>

*"Words are timeless.  You should utter them or write them with a knowledge of their timelessness."*

*-Kahlil Gibran*

I learned at an early age about the language of time.  I would write sentences without proper action words and my teachers and parents would ask me, "What did they do?  If I would write a sentence without punctuation, they would ask me, "Where does this sentence end and the next begin?"  I was in first and second grade and was already subconsciously learning how important the language of time was. I learned that every complete sentence should convey time in at least three different ways. One, you should be able to tell what tense, (past, present, or future) the sentence is expressing.

Every sentence should have an action word. Verbs convey time because they are actions and every action has a time horizon. Next, every sentence ends in punctuation. Punctuation controls the speed at which we read and speak written language. This concept is important because it begins the process of thinking of time in the words and language we speak. It allows your brain

14

to see time from various different angles. Expressly for that reason, I will not be using any charts. Charts distract the eyes and cause fixation on numbers. That is the complete opposite of what I'm intending to do. What I'm attempting to do is to get you to see time in your words, thoughts and through practice, and to recognize the time implications of the words we speak.

In our language nouns and adjectives are very much time descriptors also. For example, in the sentence, "Corey is a 40 year old man." there are three time descriptors. "Is" tells the tense, which is current.  Forty is a time descriptor telling you approximately how many trips around the sun have been completed and man is a descriptor that also tells you that I have at least 18 trips around the sun, since I'm American.

All of the titles we give ourselves and others convey time. If I call someone a Pastor, you will automatically assume that they spend time with the Bible.  If I call someone an Auto Mechanic, you will assume they spend time with cars.

The same applies if I call someone a janitor.  You will assume that person spends a reasonable amount of time cleaning.  This applies to negative language as well.  If I call someone poor you assume they spend the vast majority of time with little or no money. If I call someone a welfare queen you'd assume they don't work and welfare pays all of their bills. The same applies if I call someone a slut, a whore, a nigger, or any other sort of derogatory name.

Each one of those monikers have time connotations attached to them. When or if I see you do something that doesn't match my notion of how I perceive you to spend your time, you become a liar, a phony, fake and any other number of judgements about how you spend your time.

When Ben Carson says that slavery was immigration, in a functional sense, that sentence doesn't lie. The lie by omission is that it's an inaccurate way to describe HOW they spent that time migrating. Words are important, but the context in which words are said, when words are said, and who says those words are just as important. We have to be especially careful not to let time descriptors create false flags and mislead us. For example, when you blame a poor person for being poor, not getting more education or a better job, you imply that while the job they do is a necessary function, whoever does that job SHOULD be poor. When you see something written or hear someone say that Muslims are terrorists, Black people are lazy, or Chinese people are smart, those things are very general and could be true in small proportions. We have to focus language to be more specific, using accurate time descriptors to help provide some level of context to words and language in general. How we describe each other is probably the mitigating factor in all of our verbal and written discourse. How we perceive our time descriptors of one another is basically how we interact with one another. For example, if I call you a friend, we'll most likely talk to each other politely and meet each other when we can. If I call you my girlfriend/boyfriend, that time will more likely be spent doing romantic things like dating or cuddling. I could go on and on, but the point is, the way we PERCEIVE how other people spend their time plays a major role in how we address them. A couple of quick examples; if I call person 'A' a rich person and person 'B' a poor person when I introduce them to you, your reaction is naturally going to be different. There is a natural inclination to think the rich person spends more time studying or is the more 'important' person when the only real difference in those time monikers is the amount of time their resource pool provides.

 Second example: I used to be part owner of a little dive bar.  I used to sit at the bar with a drink in hand and buy drinks just like other patrons.  If you didn't know me you would think of me like anybody else in that space.  On quite a few nights I would buy guys and gals drinks, especially if they had bought a few already.  I did this without any fanfare; just a tip of the cap and raising of my glass.  When the people thought I was a patron like them I would get half assed smiles and an occasional thank you.  When they found out I was an owner the dudes wanted to pitch me ideas for the bar and the ladies thought it was a marriage proposal.  It was silly how different the reactions were to my action when their concept of how I spent my time changed.  So when you talk about people, be careful about what time descriptors you give them.  Also, when being addressed, you have to be careful of the time descriptors that people use to describe you.  You know how you spend your time and the most accurate time descriptors to be used when you're being addressed.  Our challenge is to come to some kind of common ground about how we address one another, and time descriptors, while not perfect, will draw a baseline for how we relate.

## Time Lessons:

Time is in everything we say and do.

# **Time and Education**

*"People think of education as something they can finish"*

*-Isaac Asimov*

The way the American education system is set up for the vast majority of people, formal academic career determines adult employment opportunities.  Time shows us that your formal education is one of your most important time descriptors.   With that being said, I thank my mentors for showing me about how education determines how you spend your time.  My formal education in school settings taught me that the better you doin these formal settings, the better the opportunities that will be available to you. There are fundamental things you must learn in your formal education, like how to understand the written word and how to do basic mathematics. Up until 8th grade, I spent 95% percent of my time sleeping, eating, reading, or playing sports. The other part of time was spent traveling or talking to my elders. When I got to high school and my academic attention span faded, so did my opportunities. I had the test scores to go to any college in the country, but my grades were just good enough to pass. That mediocrity cost me an opportunity to go to my first choice school and to play college football. I started to get negative time monikers attached to my name and because I did, it affected my relationship with the staff and teachers at school. Counselors were in no rush to give me recommendations. Teachers were in no rush to help me when I needed it. That was entirely my fault though, and to this day those behaviors cost me time and money. I got accepted to a bunch of colleges because of the high school I went to and my test scores, but those colleges offered me no scholarships or any other financial aid. I was forced to take out loans that I am still repaying to this very day. That lack of attention to detail in my formative years has cost me tens of thousands of dollars to date and will no doubt end up costing me hundreds of thousands of dollars as time goes on.  What it costs me in dollars, it also cost me in time.  Each one of those dollars could and should be going towards any number of things that could save me time or make the time I have here more pleasurable.

And that's just one example.   This same thing happens to a lot of people.  They let their wants get in the way of their educational needs.  Or even worse they don't know they have educational needs.  The bottom line is that your formal education time moniker is a

HUGE determining factor in how much money and how many opportunities are provided for you and to you. Lack of money means you will have to work longer hours just to have the basic creature comforts like shelter, clothing and water. Lack of education also leaves you more vulnerable to living in highly policed areas without the ability to move, which leaves you more vulnerable to going to jail. The least educated among us are more vulnerable to all of the shady parts of society because they are not in the positions to properly defend themselves because they just don't know or they just don't want to know. Either way, the time you lose to ignorance is immeasurable. If your perceived time moniker is poor or uneducated or worse, both, you lose opportunities and therefore time. We all know a few people who defy these odds. We also know large swaths of the population that fit this description. We all know what's possible. Our job is to turn possible to probable.

One of the ways to change the time moniker of uneducated is to become an expert at something. Because we live in an economy that is extremely capitalistic, you need to be able to apply that level of expertise to a venture. Most people do this by going to school.

Schools give you a piece of paper that says you have spent "x" amount of time with a subject, helping you to shed your negative time moniker because someone can vouch for your time. There are other ways to show mastery and expertise without formal schooling.

Skills and trades require great amounts of practice but not necessarily formal schooling. Games like poker and basketball take great mathematic skill and long hours to be great. Artists, craftsman, politicians, writers, entrepreneurs or however you choose to spend your time, spend it becoming an expert. Time in leads to results out. Think Tiger Woods and Serena

Williams.  Not spending time to educate yourself is a sure way to have someone else leverage your time.  Information always has been and always will be the currency of the affluent.  If you don't remember anything else I tell you, remember this:  THE PERSON THAT INFORMS THE MARKET, CONTROLS THE MARKET.  Period.  It is why our government works so hard to keep us confused and dumb.  It is why Google, Facebook, and Tesla are light years ahead of other companies.  It is how gurus become gurus.  It why the Vegas sports book rarely loses money.  So when I say expert, I mean the person that informs the market.  You become the person that does something so well that people seek you out. And this is not just talking about your formal education. It also goes for your traveling education and your environmental education. All of the functions of education are important if we are to fight against losing time. The first thing we must recognize, is that a lack of knowledge is costing us. I was told as a child that ignorance is the most expensive thing in the world. And what ignorance costs you is time. Time is the one thing you cannot get back.

Speaking of time you cannot get back, mentorship is something we need to provide, and take advantage of when provided. Mentorship in education is like a time gateway. You get to experience success at a greater rate without losing the time it costs to make all of the mistakes the person that mentored you made. It is also a way to speed up your educational progress by having someone walk you through all of the processes. We lose time because we don't seek mentorship. Mentorship should be at the forefront of our time sharing and time saving educational processes if we want to shed our negative time monikers more quickly. A mentor is somebody who has put in the time and can vouch for you doing the same; someone that has expertise and can confer that expertise to you and communicate that your time expenditure is/was valid.   Also without mentorship you may not know what you are doing wrong which could cost you valuable time and resources.  As I like to say, "do it correctly or be doomed to do it repeatedly", a version of my 6th grade Teacher Mr. Thompson's philosophy, "do it right or do it over".  We have forums where we can mentor in group settings now.  So there really is no excuse.  We can begin to address some of the causes of the time it costs us to have these negative monikers attached to our name due to a lack of education.

This can be done by validating one another through mentorship and through our intentional, organized economic and academic support of one another.

**Time Lessons:**

Pay attention to your formal education. Being ignorant will cost you a lot of time.

Become an expert at something. Time in equals results out.

THE PERSON THAT INFORMS THE MARKET, CONTROLS THE MARKET!

Mentorship is a key time saving tool. We can validate one another.

# Social Issues and Time

*"Governments want efficient technicians not human beings, because human beings become dangerous to governments – and to organized religions as well.  That is why governments and religious organizations seek to control education."*

*-Jiddu Krishnamurti*

If we want to discuss lost time as it pertains to social issues we cannot ignore American Slavery.  It is the foundational concept upon which the leveraging of time for resources (hyper capitalism) is built. Outside of hyper capitalism, other heinous parts of American Slavery still functionally exist. Those parts are nourished, fed, encouraged by the form of capitalism that American Slavery unleashed upon the world. The model created by American Slavery was mastered by the American slave owner and replicated around the globe. American Slavery literally built the economy of the world we live in today and its concepts still informs the decision making processes of our nation (America) and many others around the globe.

Social problems at their core, are about how we spend our time and how we define the way we spend our time. We have been lied to and distracted. The function of our government has never changed. Functionally, the rules of our government were put together by a set of rich European dudes to protect them from a bunch of rich European dudes. The way it looks over the years has changed some but the original functionality has NEVER changed. The speed of social change moves at the speed of the dominant culture and only when it disrupts the economic harmony of rich White dudes. Don't believe me...I'm not even going to go back to the 14, 15, and 1600s. I will start with the signing of the Articles of Confederation in 1776. White women, the people who bear and raise the children, did not by law, have the right to vote until 1920. 1-9-2-0. Nearly 150 years after the document was signed. In that time, a whole Civil War and World War was fought. Black men, former slaves, and indigenous men had the right to vote before White women. If they don't care about them, what in the world makes you think they care about YOU? Another example is the 13th Amendment to the Constitution that was signed into law and supposedly gave Black folks their freedom. 75 years of

Jim Crow later and 13, yes 13 Constitutional Amendments later we finally had the same illusion of freedom that the average White man has had since 1776. This was in the 1970's. Damn near 200 years from 1776 and more than 110 years AFTER we were "freed" by the 13th Amendment to the Constitution. At no time did rich White dudes stop being in charge, at no time did the government stop invading foreign countries, at no time did the government stop leveraging our time for their own gain, at no time did anything that functionally makes our government our government stop happening. As a 40 year old man with a mother in her

60's I was a few years from being alive when Black folks didn't have all the supposed civil liberties provided by the U.S. Constitution. My mother lived to be an adult without these rights. It's 2-0-1-7!!! If you think about that, my generation was the first one in U.S. history to experience what is supposed to be relative equity from birth. And I'm 40! Not 60, 70, 100, 150; 4-0! So when we are talking about the speed of social change in America we have to talk about what that means structurally and functionally. We are fighting the tentacles. The foundation is built on the economic principle of leveraging your time for resources and so to actually affect change we need to think in terms of taking back our time, our most valuable resource. We need to stop being so reactionary and build. It's been proven over time that social movements are only effective when they are backed by economic ones. Black folks have had very few sustained economic movements that have not been co-opted by or sold to White folks. No amount of marching means anything to a country that was built on the slaughtering of the indigenous population through Manifest Destiny and that was built economically on the African Slave Trade. There is a direct correlation between our economic ineptitude as a whole and our diminished status in the eyes of America and the world. Every group, nationality, and race besides us Black Americans is buying and selling their politics and politicians and we are on the sidelines taking a principled stand getting the shit slapped out of us. This country was built on our time being leveraged by our oppressors and is still being run by that same system and we are marching and rioting instead of connecting and building. Every second we spend ASKING for social justice is a wasted second. Time has shown us repeatedly that when we work together that the government has to spend time listening.

Black Wall Street, the Harlem
Renaissance, the Black Panthers, and
the UNIA proved in just the last 100
years that if we work together we don't
need to ASK for anything.  The
government has spent years
brainwashing us and feeding us literal
bullshit to keep us from realizing the
power of our unified time.

One of the biggest weapons the
government uses to occupy our time and
resources is criminality.  Making things
illegal and then creating negative time
monikers to go with the passing of
criminal laws is the way to keep
American Slavery functional by just

changing its form. One of the misnomers about jails and criminality is that they "give you time"; Nope! They take time from you. The world as you knew it will never exist the same way again. The people you love change, the technology advances, the world moves on. They use it as a way to invalidate accomplishment. They use it as a way to create a negative time experience for you and to boost the productivity of themselves and big corporations. Nothing about criminality is about giving you anything. They threaten to control your body in order to control your thoughts and actions. Hell, they use it to boost populations to control political situations and capital. Jails check all the boxes of a hyper-capitalist society; free or low cost labor with little to no thought to condition, replaceable labor, controlling the length of work day, and being able to track and control the bodies of your work population when they are not working. And with the advance of technology, the stigma of criminality never goes away, creating a feedback loop of recidivism.

The criminal justice system also acts as a secondary form of taxation for the majority of citizens. Tickets and fines are issued for infractions that fill the coffers of government. We haven't even begun to talk about the primary taxation which funds the government. For the average person, refusal to pay these taxes can result in the imprisonment (stealing of your time) by the government. Functionally, the average person in America is in the same social situation as a peasant in 13th century England or any European country from 800 years ago.

The constant threat of criminality, taxation, inflation, stagnant wages and the rising costs of living are all forms of time scarcity, causing you to work longer and get less stuff. Capitalism in this form devalues the human experience and makes it a perfect vehicle for control.  The government and large companies are in a rush to gather and then distribute your information as broadly as possible to inform their decisions about how to further devalue your time.  Remember, the person (entity) that informs the market, controls it.  Every industry is built around the transference of your time capital into their resource capital.  Life Insurance, health insurance, advertising, oil, electronics, you name it.  They keep you in front of fake news stories so that real ones get lost.  They will share your health information and your online habits.  They already track your commute to work and control the length of your work day. We are being constantly bombarded and the thing that ties these bombardments together is time and the governmental lust to control it. Knowing that someone is manipulating your time is actually comforting to some. For those of us that would like a little free will with our coffee, a little self-determination, it's infuriating. The crazy part about real capitalism is that nobody or no entity would be too big to fail. If a person, company, or even our government becomes so insolvent that it can't do the business it was intended to do, then another entity would replace it and those that invested in that entity would take that "L". Our government has been insolvent for YEARS in many different ways and we haven't done a single thing to redirect or change the function since its inception. Our time is THEIR money. We just keep feeding the pig.

**Time Lessons:**

Social change happens when economic change happens.

The U.S. government is built by using your time for their resources.

Every second you spend asking for social change is a wasted second.

If we want something to change, we have to change it.  Stop feeding the pig.

# <u>Lifespan and Time</u>

*"What type time you on?"*

*-Any Average Philadelphian*

Time is the resource that makes all other resources possible. There are lots of ways to measure time and one way is the span between life and death. Life being the beginning, whether measured from conception or birth and death being the final chapter.

Life can be measured in moments and let's talk about some of these moments. The average person gets between 80 and 90 years the way our current system is set up. That's something like 29,000 to 33,000 days. That's it. No one is guaranteed these days. Approximately 1/3 of these days is going to be spent sleeping, so even if you make it to be 90 you are going to spend approximately 30 years recuperating. So my assertion is that it is not life, but death that is our muse and inspiration. Death is the thing that powers us. It gives us a sense of urgency that immortality would take from us. Because of its finality as the end of our conscious time, it makes the 24 hours we spend in each day an urgent sprint and not a leisurely walk.

We need to talk about how we spend these days and who we spend these days with. In some cities, Black folks have lifespans that are 15-25 years shorter than our White counterparts. That's thousands of days we don't get to spend with our family, our friends, or chasing our goals. Wasted time is wasted opportunity. Take the time to love those that are close to you. Memories > stuff.

Having said that, we also need to do things during our lifespan that make it so the next generation of Black people don't start at zero. We need to build things that last outside of our last day. While gaining knowledge and getting degrees is important and necessary you can't give them to your kids or spouse or family. People will always remember how you make them feel and love is nice but poverty is CRUSHING. We need to get things like life insurance. We need to own stock in companies or own a company that can be passed to our progeny. We need to build/create things that have material value that can be redeemed in the world. While the wealth gap is realized during life, it is started at death. No matter what survey or study about insurance or inheritance you look at we get paid less and we get paid less often. The time advantage of being able to have resources you don't have to work for is immeasurable.

We also need to take better care of our health.  Health is a major time issue because it not only determines how many days you spend here but the quality of those days.  Poor health due to stress, poor diet, lack of exercise, and lack of awareness is a major contributory factor to why our lifespan as Black people in America is so much shorter than the average person.  The specter of death hanging over our community also makes us think in short term strategies and not in long term strategies that will benefit us and our families.  It's hard to think about building long term generational wealth or taking any long term strategy like a

401k or Roth IRA when you can't see your life past the day you are living in. I know this firsthand. I never thought I would live to be 21. 30 was a pipe dream. 40 was a rumor. I only started thinking long term when I had children.

The inability to take long term positions makes it hard for us to build. Long term positions are legacy positions. They are about using the leverage of time to help to build resources. Long term positions usually take the cooperation of more than one person over long periods of time. Black folk need long term positions to go with our daily grind. It is the thing that will allow for growth, and change. For example: I own stocks and collections and I also have life insurance. I am part owner in 3 different businesses and I have written this book. All of these things will outlive me. My job is to teach my children how to grow and manage these things. That is the long term position.

**Time Lessons:**

Life is short. Death is coming. Memories >Stuff.

Health is wealth. Stuff is important. Think outside your lifespan.

# Religion Over Time

*"Do actions agree with words?*
*There's your measure of reliability.*
*Never confine yourself to the words."*

*-Frank Herbert*

I was raised Baptist in a neighborhood with 4 Baptist Churches within 1 block of my house. There were a few prevailing themes with all the churches:

1.    The building fund. Tithe until it hurts because we need a new building.

2.    Jesus is King. Believe or go to hell.

3.     The end of days is near.  Get prayed up.

There were also a large amount of Muslims in my neighborhood and a few mosques within walking distance of my house also.  There were a few common themes with the Muslims in my neighborhood:

1.     They were really sensitive about any perceived slander of Islam.  Perceived or real transgressions could get ugly; verbally or physically.

2.     Allah is God. Mohammed is the prophet. Believe or go to hell.

3.    The bean pies were
SPECTACULAR.  The Final Call is a
dope piece of literature.  Their building
fund is way tastier and entertaining than
tithing.

Special shout out to the Hebrew
Israelites that used to set up on busy
street corners with speakers and mega
phones to get their message out and to
the Jehovah's Witnesses that used to
wake me up on the weekend knocking
on my door like the Sheriff's
department serving a search warrant.

I have A LOT of thoughts on Black
folks and religion.  All the thoughts I
share here are related to time.  I'm

going to preface this list by saying I love you anyway!!

1.     Religion might be the biggest waste of time in the history of Black America.  THE BIGGEST.   As a matter of fact, you were Black before you were any religion that was given to you or chosen by you.  Before you had consciousness you had your genetic makeup.  But you will deny your heritage and claim religion.  That's ass backwards.  And it's a major reason we can't build.  You spend time on these rituals that are supposed to unify you.  Then you spend time beefing with anybody that doesn't believe in the

same rituals that you do.  That's like beefing because one person has on a red tee and another has on a blue one (wink, wink).  How about this…We have been on this continent by force and then by choice for roughly 500 years.  We have had plenty of time to create and establish our own cultural norms.  Yet we spend time edifying some invisible deities and praying and wishing for stuff that we HAVE CONTROL OVER!  Talk about wasting time…

2.	ALL God stories are a waste of time.  THEY DON'T CHANGE OUTCOMES!  We try to put ourselves above the rest of the Universe when we are EXACTLY like the rest of the Universe. Our ego won't let us believe that we are born and die like every other living thing in the Universe and that when we die our energy and consciousness die with us. We are dispersed or dispatched as the Universe sees fit. You're not that special. Get over yourself. Our time is dictated by our species or living classification like everything else.

3.    If we took the money we put into religion and put it into building viable businesses that actually serve and employ people, we wouldn't be waiting on a savior. There is a direct correlation

between business ownership and crime; between business ownership and educational outcomes; between business ownership and political and social outcomes.  We have been waiting for a savior for hundreds of years and that hasn't worked once.  NOT ONE TIME.  When are we going to realize that our futures are tied to us unifying in business, and not having a house party with religious music and wishing for change?

4.     I don't want religions or religious institutions dissolved.  I just think they are inefficient.  Over time they have proven ineffective in creating

meaningful change. Why do you think the Government dismantled the Black Panthers and burned down Black Wall Street or charged Garvey with all kinds of crimes to break up the UNIA while leaving the thousands of Black churches making billions of dollars a year standing? If the church was really a unifying force, don't you think that the Government would smash and dismantle that too?

5.     When you "give God the glory" you are doing yourself a major disservice. Or when you say, "It was God's will" you absolve yourself from personal responsibility. That's like

telling your kids that Santa bought their birthday present.  Or that the Easter bunny brought their school clothes.  Naw son!  Check this out- I'm fat.  I don't exercise enough and I like cheesesteaks.  So is it God's will that I be fat?  If I get up at 4:30 a.m. every morning and run and work out and get in shape am I supposed to give God all the glory?  I'm fat because I made/make bad decisions and if I get in shape it will be because I busted my ass to make sure it happens.  It devalues your/my time and efforts and makes ZERO sense to give the glory to "God", unless you consider yourself to be God.  But whatever.  What is wrong with taking credit for a job well done?  What's wrong with taking responsibility for your actions good or bad or with building with your brothers and sisters?  It wasn't God's will. It was YOUR will.  You got up and did it.  OWN IT! You put the time in.  That time is valuable.  Don't give it away to lack of confidence.  Self-determination in the singular form and the plural form is a concrete goal we can set for ourselves.  You can't believe in personal accountability and still believe that some mystical, mythical force is controlling your every movement, can you?  C'MON SON!  You can believe in a Creator without believing this hocus pocus.

6.     I will work with you if you are Christian, Jewish, Muslim, Hindu, Atheist, Agnostic, or any of the 5000 or so recognized religions. IDGAF.  We have to build.  I'm not about to let a difference in worshiping philosophy keep me from helping my brothers and sisters.  You shouldn't either.

7.     You are allowed to vehemently disagree with me.  I don't care if you like or dislike what you read here.  I love you anyway.  Hard truths > Pretty Lies.

**Time Lessons:**

Heritage > Religion.

Get over yourself.

Viable Businesses > Religious institutions.

Be confident.

Hard Truths > Pretty Lies.

# Price vs. Value

*"It costs me nothing to pay you no mind."*

*-Jay-Z*

The ability to evaluate the price of an item versus its value is a premier time saving skill. Price is easily determined. With a product or service price is usually given at the time of purchase and your experience with the product or service will determine the value. For example: if you buy a pair of Air Jordans the price will normally be between $120 and $240 dollars retail.

Depending on what pair you get and what you plan on doing with them they have a value of $300 to $500 on the secondary market. If you wear them the value for resale goes down, but if you're happy with the purchase then the value to you, personally, still remains high.

The variable most people miss when talking about price and value is time. Time figures in, in a variety of ways. In terms of price, time figures into the price when making and delivering the product. With value you have to figure how much time you have to spend and what actions you have to take, to get the value you want versus the price of your product.

Price vs. Value also applies to relationships. When evaluating relationships I ALWAYS do a price analysis. What is spending time with this person going to cost me? Is it worth the time I'm going to spend? Am I willing to pay the price to maintain this relationship? What is the time horizon of this relationship? What do I bring to the table? What do I need to make this relationship work? Can I help them? Can they help themselves? There are at least 20-30 questions I ask within a few seconds of meeting a person.  Price vs. Value reaches all areas of your life.

Along with price vs. value analysis we all need to do inventory of our wants versus our needs.  Make a simple T chart.  On the left side of the chart write your schedule in as much detail as possible.  On the right side write the things that you want.  All of them.  Spending more time with friends, vacations, a simple nap.  All of it.  Then begin to move the things from the right side of the column into the left side.  Literally make time to do the things you want to do.  When you write your schedule down you will probably find out a few things.  One thing is that you probably waste a bunch of time.  We all do.  Another thing is that you can't account for all of your time, even if you tried.  The last thing you'll notice is that you probably aren't making a lot of time to do the things you want to do.  If you are honest with yourself about what you want and you make the time to do those things you can't help but be happier.

**Time Lessons:**

Price vs. Value is a critical time saver.

Do not forget time in your analysis.

Make the time to do the things you want to do.

# Time and Technology

*"As technology advances in complexity and scope, fear becomes more primitive"*

*-Don DeLillo*

Time and technology have a complicated relationship.  On one hand, technology has made the world smaller than it's ever been and created businesses with low barriers to entry.  On the other hand, we have the ability to kill just about every living thing because the technology is so powerful.  Technology has enhanced and sped up our lives in so many ways it's hard to count.  From the cotton gin to the microprocessor, technology creates time for us that we wouldn't otherwise have.  Technology also causes some to lose time because it either becomes a crutch or a distraction.

What you and I must do is keep up with technological advances and monitor them to make sure that we don't become obsolete.  Technology is part of our ecosystem and we need to treat it as such.  It is both predator and prey.  Do you remember catalogs like Montgomery Ward? How about when Avon was the hottest thing in the streets?  K-mart?  Now you can go to sites like E-Bay or Amazon and scoop anything these previous places could provide.  Do you remember sky pagers and cell phones as big as a car battery?  Rotary phones?  Phone booths?  Now your cell phone is a laptop, camera, phone booth, house phone, library, and a partridge and a pear tree.

Technology can also be a HUGE time waster.  Hell, I used to play Madden like it was my full time job.  There was also a time when I used to play between 4,000 and 10,000 hands a day of Texas Hold'em on a computer.  I've ended Zelda, Castlevania, Ninja Gaiden, and

Contra. I still go on Facebook to write a status and end up watching 20 minutes of video. Bottom line, don't get caught up in technology so much that it interferes with your ability to reach your goals. Use technology, don't let it use you.

**Time Lessons**:

Technology is part of our ecosystem. Respect it.

Don't get distracted.

# Random Thoughts about

# Time

*WIIIIIILD OOOOUTTTT!!!*

*-LOX BARZ*

These thoughts probably belong somewhere in this body of work.  So, here we go:

1.      There is nothing wrong with linear income; which is the income directly related to the number of hours you work.  Whatever you have to do to get the results you prefer is alright with me.  But if linear income is all you have you will be more vulnerable to your

employer's whims.  Invest in SOMETHING.  Anything.  Get some income that is not tied to your primary source of income.  Something that pays interest over time or adds value over time like stocks, property, or collections to name a few.  It frees your mind and your time.

2.    Pool your resources.  Find a small group of people you trust.  Share. Seems really simple on paper. REEEEEALY hard to do in reality.

3.    Do it in increments.  A drip given enough time will become a flood.  The more people you can find to drip with

you, the less time it takes to become a flood.

4.     Build systems.  Systems allow more people to participate.  They allow for duplicate work from different people.  They allow people that have never participated to participate at a higher level.  Systems are time savers and legacy builders.

5.     What gets measured gets done.  One of the reasons I know religion wastes time is that the stated goal of salvation isn't measurable.  McDonald's can tell you exactly how many burgers they sold yesterday.  Your religious institution will never be able to produce

a spreadsheet that tells you how many souls they save or reincarnated. Never. The only two things religious institutions can count are followers and money. They're like Instagram. Set goals. Then create a way to measure whether or not you are reaching those goals.

6.    Reduce your exposure to people and environments that are not conducive to your improvement. This is another easy one to write and hard one to do. The key to this one is proper goal setting. If you are constantly in places or around people that do not help you

accomplish anything, you need to bounce.

7.    Help as many people as you can. You will learn lots of things that will save you time over time. You will also help a lot of people.

8.    We are not robots. Make time for love and happiness and fun. Those things are part of the experience that make the other stuff worth the time you will spend doing them.

   I'm out here. Get at me.

# _Part II: Own Your SPACE_

## _By_

## _Jimmy_

# My Relationship With Space

*"On the head of a man or woman that believes in themselves a worthless rag can become a 10 million dollar fashion item"*

*-KRS One*

I have always had a relationship with space. Space has always represented freedom to me. When I was a teenager space represented freedom. Now, as a grown a$$ man space still represents freedom. The way I see freedom has changed though. As a kid, I wanted my own space like every kid does. I remember it being a big deal to get my own room filled with my own things. Of course I didn't own anything but that space, even if it was temporary was a sign of freedom and independence. In fact, I remember getting my own phone in my own room and I thought I was really doing something.

As an adult I have a deeper understanding of how important space is. It's one of the reasons I started BuyTheHood.com, which is a newsletter and live lecture series that teaches the importance of saving, investing, and using real estate as a tool of empowerment. I got tired of hearing people say "I want to make it out of the hood" or "I'm getting out of the hood". Don't get me wrong I'm not knocking people for having that mentality. Live and let live. What I'm saying is I want to try and improve "The Hood". I want to show people the beauty of what we already have access to. It reminds me of an old story one of my mentors told me called Acres of Diamonds. This story was a part of a lecture given by Russell Conwell who is the founder and first president of Temple University. Anyone who rides down Broad Street in Philadelphia will see that Temple University understands the power of

space.  Back to "Acres of Diamonds"…
Conwell tells a story about an African
farmer who was so desperate to find
diamonds that he sold off his farm to go
off and search for them.  He never
found the diamonds and ended up
committing suicide. Meanwhile the new
owner of his property found a very rich
diamond mine right on the farm.   The
point is, sometimes the opportunity or
fortune you think you have to leave to
find is something you have access to
right now but you don't recognize it.  I
want people to see the diamond that is
the hood.  Don't move out of the hood!
 Fix The Hood!  Space can be a tool for
you to do so.

# Space and Education

*"I'd be lying if I said I didn't want millions, more than money saved I want to save children."*

*-Common*

I don't want to sound all "Rich Dad Poor Dad" but we aren't educated about the power or importance of space. For the most part we are taught to be workers and become part of a system. When we are exposed to anything else such as the arts, politics, entrepreneurship, etc we aren't made aware of how space is a factor.

I remember when I was a young man getting ready to head to college to earn a degree in political science. My plan was to help my people through the political process. After my first year of classes I worked on some campaigns and recognized how politics worked on a local level in Philadelphia. I saw how those who made the donations received access and used that access to push their agenda. I started doing research on the people making the donations. What I learned was those who made the most donations and had the most "juice" were those that owned space. It didn't matter whether they were Doctors, Lawyers, Accountants, Preachers, Businessmen, etc.  Even if they had a career they would ultimately acquire space and grow wealth from the space they owned.  That's what got me interested in the real estate business.

While studying the appraisal of real estate, I learned many economic principles.  The one that I will always remember is what economist call the "Agents of Production".   The agents of production discuss what factors are crucial to our economy because they are what is needed to produce all goods and services.  Those agents are land, labor, capital, and entrepreneurship.

The first agent, land includes any natural resource used to produce goods and services. What's interesting about that is I remember one of my mentors telling me that owning space is the best investment in the world because it is the natural resource with the easiest barrier to entry. That is powerful. You have to first think about what a natural resource is. I don't care if you are a Bible thumper, whether you believe in the theory of evolution, the big bang theory, or if you're a "flat earther", the one thing they would all probably agree on is as long as humans have lived on this earth they have depended on things that exist in nature to survive, such as water, land, soils, animals, minerals, fossil fuels, rocks, and forests/vegetation. When you look at these natural resources you'll notice in order to create something with the others you will still need space/land to do so.

The second agent of production, labor, relates to the effort or wages that people contribute to goods and services. This can be direct or indirect. The third agent, capital, is the cost of obtaining money to produce. This could be from a bank, venture capital, or many other sources. The last agent entrepreneurship, is the process of putting everything together to produce an item.

These agents come into play when producing anything. This is an example of how important land is and why owning land will always remain important. No matter what your business is land will be a factor. Once I fully understood these agents my idea of how important space is changed forever. I realized owning space can be just as important to a doctor, mechanic, or pharmacist as it could be to a real estate investor. When I talk about education as it relates to owning space, I'm not talking about telling you how to buy land or properties with no money down. I want you to think about space/land in a completely different way. I want you to understand that not only does land/space have, but why it has value. I run into people all the time who own space and they end up losing it or not maximizing it because they don't know why it's valuable. They know they should own it because they watched an infomercial, saw multiple HGTV shows or clicked on a paid Facebook ad, but they don't understand the value. Once you grasp the four agents of production you will understand that land = power and Lil Kim has taught us that power is one of the three keys to life.

# Social Issues and Space

*"They got money for wars but can't feed the poor."*

*-Tupac Shakur*

There are people who understand the power in owning your space and the importance in owning your space. However, many don't understand the connection between space and how it impacts social issues. I love books. In fact S/O to Pizza Hut for allowing me to combine two of the loves of my life with the Book It! program back in elementary school. For those who have no clue about what I'm referring to, the

"Book It!" program gave kids free pizza for reading a specific number of books. I believe #PizzaIsLife and I also love books so salute to Pizza Hut although your Pizza is actually trash. At any rate, I read a couple books that completely changed my relationship with space. Those books are "Family Properties" by Beryl Satter and "The History of Great American Fortunes" by Gustavas Myers. Salute to Byron another 254 brother for recommending Family Properties.

*Family Properties* discusses the segregation in the beautiful city of Chicago in the 1950's and 1960's.

Through this book I came to learn about how laws and fear mongering were used to segregate and control the space which allowed families to obtain political, and economic control over the city and the environment. There are neighborhoods that have been plagued with crime and poverty for years but it's not a reflection of the residents but a reflection of how systems were put in place to control the space. This is not ignoring personal responsibility but if you understand history and how space was used as a negative mechanism of control you will better understand how to use space as a way to get control from a positive standpoint.

*The History of Great American Fortunes* gave me an account of the land speculators of Dutch and British America and how they used land to amass fortunes.  The wealth created by owning the space led to corruption of the political process and the exploitation of workers and the overall working class.

Now I could give you an entire history lesson on how redlining created what we know as ghettos or how many White families built "spite fences" when African Americans moved close to them, or how the prison industrial complex uses land to keep minorities enslaved but what I want to concentrate on is how we can use the ownership of space for a positive social change.

Many people will get to this part and think "Damn Jimmy, I don't own any space and I copped this book thinking you would tell me how. Well in the words of Big Red "my office hours are from 9 to 5".  Also I will give you some advice later in the book but anytime I get to reference The Five Heartbeats I have to do so.  Owning space can make a positive impact by creating communities.  That includes more than just residential buildings.  When I say community I also mean gardens, businesses, art studios etc. If you are waiting for the government to do these things then you will be waiting for a while. It is up to us to come together and create environments that promote positivity and stimulate innovation. Owning space creates a capital base which is essential to creating jobs, and becoming a force politically. *Family Properties* discusses how in the past, lending institutions didn't mind loaning Black Americans money for a car but didn't want to lend them money to buy land. The book states that a Wall Street Journal Reporter was told "Within the system there is a willingness to lend all you need to buy a car". "A car can't appreciate…. When you want to buy a house, however, you get only a big frown…. The house represents a method of capital appreciation in the ghetto community. And a strong capital base is a threat to the white community."

Now, I know that many people are still waiting on their 40 Acres and a mule, but we have to stop waiting and start doing! Land can be an important part of social change if we understand how to use it to create a capital base.

# Price vs Cost vs Value

*"The best investment on earth is earth."*

*-Louis Glickman*

I speak with people about real estate and space/land on a daily basis and have done so for the last 20 years. I realized a long time ago that many people confuse price with value. There is also confusion about how cost relates to price and value. A simple explanation is price the amount paid to get something. It's the actual number of dollars a service or product garners.

That means price is a fact and not a theoretical concept. Cost is the amount of money or resources it takes to produce a good. Value is the worth of a product/service for an individual and is more of a theoretical concept than a fact. Value is important though and can change based on what kind of value we're talking about.

Now what does this have to do with "Owning Your Space" you ask? Follow along and you will soon understand why I'm explaining these concepts. First you have objective value which is a belief that something has value because it exists. This belief emphasizes cost. Then there is subjective value which is a belief that like beauty, value is in the eye of the beholder. For example, take a key to your house. I know it has value because it exists as a key (Objective Value) and it may have minimal value to me because I have no use for it. To you the key has a different value (Subjective) because it allows you to gain access to your home and if you lose the key, you would have to replace it which takes time and by now you know how valuable that is.

This is the reason I believe owning your space is important. I don't believe that everyone is meant to be a homeowner. Don't get me wrong; that is a personal preference and there are strategies that make perfect sense that involve renting. You can however still own space while being a tenant.

Gentrification has been a hot button topic in recent years and has been a topic of discussion for decades and I make people aware that owning your space is a way to fight gentrification (if you consider it a negative). The "Buy The Hood" movement has been a success because it has allowed me to help people understand the real value in doing so. Owning your "hood" is not about the cost or the price but about the subjective value it has to you and your overall community. Owning space makes you a stakeholder and as a stakeholder you have the ability to influence more than just the value of your space but the community as a whole. Now I'm not trying to sound like Stephen Bannon and suggest that only property owners should vote but what I am saying is there is value outside of a dollar amount that comes from owning your space.

This is a reason it hurts when I see people lose their property. This is a major issue. I speak to people all the time who are in a situation where they had a grandmother or uncle who understood the importance of ownership but the next generation loses the land due to taxes, or liens. According to Time.com 70% of rich families lose their wealth by the second generation. Imagine this number for people on the come up or those who are working or poor class. I know there is a chapter on solutions but I also wanted to mention in this chapter about value, that we need to protect those legacies and become more informed about what we are losing. This goes for space anywhere in any condition. We already talked about how it has value just because it exists, and by now (hopefully) you understand subjective value.  So now let's take a look at why sometimes not having that understanding can result in families losing valuable land.

I'm pretty sure you've talked to someone who is your elder and they talk about the cost of something when they were younger vs the cost today (thanks inflation).  You may also hear them wish they'd held onto something of value which is worth more now than it was when they first acquired it, or you may have heard the story of a lady who held onto three shares of stock and because she never sold that $180 investment turned into 7 million.  The point is buying and holding something of value can pay dividends in the long run (No Chris Rios intended). Due to social issues (like some mentioned in the previous chapter) some of our neighborhoods ended up looking like third world countries. You see some of those same neighborhoods years later and now you can't afford to live there because they have had a tremendous increase in value. Neighborhoods consistently go through life cycle stages. These stages could last for decades but they are always in one of four stages. The stages are growth, stability, decline, revitalization. This is important to remember because too many people sell or lose their space during the decline stage and are not able to participate in the revitalization. Let me break down those four stages for you. Growth is a period where the neighborhood is expanding or developing. Stability happens after growth. This usually happens after there is no more land available to build on and the neighborhood stops growing but is maintaining. After stability, decline will occur. This happens because the buildings depreciate and are not maintained. As a result the demand for an area declines and it can no longer compete with comparable neighborhoods. Here is what's amazing about this cycle.  After declining, a neighborhood will see revitalization which is when it is brought back and is given a new life.  When people are stakeholders and owners, some neighborhoods can remain in the stabilization part of the cycle for years and years because that space has tremendous value and those stakeholders make sure it never gets to the declining phase.  Now let me tie this all together.  It is imperative that you know the difference between price, cost and value.  When you do know that difference you understand how valuable owning space can be and it's not always from an economic standpoint.  If you happen to be someone who has inherited space make sure you protect it and make keeping it a priority. If you disregard it because of it's current state because you could lose it for nothing and the next thing you know it's in a different stage of the life cycle and you missed out on the benefit and then you catch the vapors.

# Big Mac & A Bible

*"We are not technically in the food business. We are in the real estate business. The only reason we sell fifteen-cent hamburgers is because they are the greatest producer of revenue, from which our tenants can pay us our rent."*

*-Former McDonald's CFO, Harry J. Sonneborn*

Big organizations have benefited from owning space since the beginning of time. Many people believe every war fought since the beginning of time has been over land. I actually believe wars are fought over resources, but even if that is true I've already told you space is needed for every other resource.  The best example I can give in regards to organizations using land to acquire power and wealth would be McDonald's and The Catholic Church.

Everyone knows what McDonald's is (not to be confused with McDowell's).  What many people do not know is that although McDonald's sells burgers, fries, and other fast food items they are really a real estate company.  Don't believe what I say go read Ray Kroc's book "Grinding It Out: The Making of McDonald's".  I know some of you are saying "Jimmy you're lucky I'm reading your book I'm not reading another". I hear you and if that's the case go watch the movie "The Founder" which also tells the McDonald's origin story. McDonald's is one of the world's greatest real estate companies and their business model is genius (FYI I am a McDonald's shareholder).

McDonald's former CFO was once quoted as saying "we are not technically in the food business. We are in the real estate business. The only reason we sell fifteen-cent hamburgers is because they are the greatest producer of revenue, from which our tenants can pay us our rent." Think about that. They have found a way to get a quality tenant and provide them with a revenue stream which will help them pay rent to McDonald's all while getting a piece of the tenant's revenue stream. Only in America! *Don King Voice*. So next time you see the golden arches I want you to understand what's really going on there besides McDonald's moving more work than Melo on Respect Life.

Another example of owning space would be the Catholic Church. Now I've heard for years that the Catholic Church owns more land than anyone and how they use it to do everything from generate revenue to hide aliens to host Illuminati meetings.  I entertain all of it because it's hilarious and I love conspiracy theories because they make the world more interesting.  I've done some research (that includes googling) and I discovered that yes the Catholic Church owns massive amounts of Space, they are the third biggest landowner in the world.  What was interesting was that as of the time of this writing, Queen Elizabeth II is number one in terms of landownership.  I'm going to need ya'll to step up ya'll United Kingdom and Royal Family conspiracies.  What's crazy about the Catholic Church and their ownership of land is that a lot of it is exempt from taxes. I'm not gonna speak on religious institutions and their contributions to the tax base because that can fill up another book and also because Corey has said enough about religious institutions to make a lot of you stop reading. In case you are still with me peep this; The Catholic Church through the ownership of space will always be valuable because of their acquisition of so much land. I've already told you about the difference between price, cost, and value but here is why that space/land will always hold value.

There is a famous Mark Twain quote that says "buy land they aren't making any more of it". This is true but it's deeper than that. Space/land has all of the characteristics of something that has value. Those characteristics are utility, scarcity, desirability, and effective purchasing power.

Utility means the product or service has the ability to satisfy a want and must have a use to someone. Scarcity means for an item to have value it is not readily available. Desirability means it is a commodity that can satisfy someone's desire, or in other words there is a demand for it.

Effective purchasing power means the commodity is able to be purchased and there is a market for it to be purchased. Land will always have these characteristics therefore it will always be valuable.

I see cats on the street say things like "This is my block" or "I rep this block". If you ask them do they own any of the space, most will say no. We need to get away from the talk of it being "our block" and start talking about how we can own the block.

# __Technology and Space__

*"Technology doesn't change people's basic needs or their natures."*

*-Priya Ardis*

You can't help but to turn on the TV or log on to your favorite social media site and see technology being discussed daily. Whether it's about a consumer product, the newest IPO, the newest game, the newest viral video, etc technology is being talked about. This has prompted many people to focus on technological fields as a profession. I think that is a beautiful thing. I think it is an amazing thing that companies like

Zillow, Air BnB, and Trulia have completely revolutionized the real estate industry. I also believe that kids should learn to code at an early age (I'm trying to learn as an old washed up man and it's not easy). What I've noticed through conversation and debate is that because of all of the technology talk many people forget that space is still important in this new world we are living in. Without the space, could Air BNB exist? Without the space what good is Zillow? If you build the next big social media platform where would you put your campus? As cloud computing becomes more of the norm where will the servers go? I am impressed by the amount of disruption that happens in Silicon Valley. I pay attention and observe that while all of these companies and brilliant people are changing the world and becoming wealthy so are the people that own the space in Silicon Valley. I follow the housing prices in those areas and it is astonishing. Many of these land owners have done nothing but hold onto the space and are now making fortunes while they sleep. The more things change, the more they stay the same. It doesn't matter whether it's the industrial revolution or a revolution in technology. Those that own the space will always be able to exercise control and exhibit power.

All of these new technologies can be used to do research and to start to acquire space. We have more information at our disposal, and more resources to help us elevate our game so it's time we make moves using this technology.

# Solutions: Don't Be A Mutombo

*"The future belongs to those who prepare for it today"*

*-Malcolm X*

This chapter can be an entire book itself. Corey gave you lessons after every chapter but I've decided to dedicate an entire chapter to solutions. My first solution is to read this book and make sure others read it as well (LOL). You have to make sure you understand just how valuable time is.

Many of my colleagues in real estate investing told me I shouldn't write about owning space because if I create new investors they will become competition. The truth is this book is more about changing your perspective than teaching you exactly how to participate, although I will give you a few pointers. Here is another secret though; I know for a fact that most people reading this book will take no action. I share my knowledge on the regular because I know most people won't take action. Most people are what I call "I'mboutoo Mutombos." I know you're wondering what that means. Well have you ever heard NBA and Strip Club legend DikembeMutombo pronounce his entire name? Also, I got so used to people telling me "I'm about to" and you see them years later and it's still "I'm about to".  I just started calling them Mutombos.  So take action.  Don't be a Mutombo.

Next we have to make sure we actually talk about money in our communities and our homes.  Money is a taboo subject for many families and IMO that is a problem.

We also have to understand it's not about how much money you make it's about how much you keep.

Working in the communities I do and sitting down with families has given me a tremendous wealth of knowledge, but has also proved many of the theories you read in books to be true. I have sat down with people who earn over 200K a year who have a lower net worth than people who work at fast food restaurants making 30K a year. It doesn't matter if you make 200K a year if you spend 201K a year trying to keep up with the Combs'.

I can hear you saying "Jimmy when are you gonna tell me anything about acquiring space?" Well here you go. If you subscribe to the

BuyTheHood.com newsletter you would already know this but in case you didn't here is a quick cuban link. In July of 2016 Curbed Philadelphia wrote an article explaining that you can buy a house in Philadelphia by saving $16 a day for 5 years.  This is based on a median sales price of $235,000 and the average down payment of 12.1 percent.  Many neighborhoods in Philadelphia have inventory selling for at least half of the median sales price in the city.  You can save $7 a day for 5 years or save the same $16 a day for a little more than 2 years to buy a property in one of those neighborhoods.

It's time to stop the talk of "getting out the hood"!  Now more than ever is the time to "Buy The Hood" and create generational wealth while improving our communities and creating better environments to live. We just explained to you that you can become a property owner by saving just $7 a day for 5 years or $16 a day for a little more than 2 years.  If you don't have it be patient. Play the long game and work up to it. This is chess not checkers.

Another solution is to not be selfish with your success.  If you have any skill or accomplishment you should share it with others.  Corey mentioned mentorship so I won't repeat it, but just know that we need to build stronger communities and that can't happen if you have success and run away or selfishly keep it to yourself.

The last thing I want to mention in regards to solutions before ending this book is to tell everyone to be prepared. What I mean by that is not only do we need to have conversations about money but we need to discuss what the next generation should do to maintain the space and time that you have worked so hard for. I mentioned earlier about how many families acquire space and it doesn't grow generationally because we lose it and end up on a treadmill. We must be prepared to have conversations about taboo subjects like money and death. People worry so much about what they will leave their kids but don't worry enough about what they leave in their kids in terms of knowledge (Barz)! We need to think generationally and know that we can have a positive social impact, while educating about space and using technology to our benefit to obtain wealth like McDonald's and create new relationships with space. See what I did there? (3-0 Bodybag)

-Jimmy

# About The Author (Corey)

Corey is North Philly born and bred. He is a sports and hip – hop junkie. Corey is college educated and yet he knows the streets are watchin'. The range of things he loves goes from board rooms to shooting dice on street corners. Known for having a quick wit and a sharp tongue, people that know him well will tell you he has matured but he has never changed. He is also known for having a special love for melanated people.

Professionally, he is an educator that specializes in working with children with emotional and intellectual disabilities.  He owns his own educational consulting business that does everything from mentoring and tutoring to auditing special education paperwork.  Corey is an investor in numerous small business projects, the stock market, and the real estate market.  In the words of the immortal Tupac Shakur, "I get around."

# About The Author (Jimmy)

Jimmy is one of The Talented Tenth, but he likes Black Timbs and Black Hoodies. He was given the nickname "The Blueprint" from a business partner years ago. He continued to use the nickname because when you search online for James Williams or Jimmy Williams millions of people come up. But, when searching for James "The Blueprint" Williams or Jimmy "The Blueprint" Williams guess who comes up?

Jimmy loves Hip Hop, Sports, Business, Books and Technology. He is also a Battle Rap Junkie. He is the Co-

Founder of War Room Sports as well as War Room Sports TV. Jimmy also buys and sells real estate in Philadelphia. In the words of the great Biggie Smalls aka Notorious B.I.G. aka Frank White aka Big Poppa aka (You Get the Point) "Game Elevates, Money I Make Into Stocks and Real Estate Bitch"....

Made in United States
Orlando, FL
03 June 2022

18461278R00085